The Incredible Kids' Craft-IT Series

Make-n-Gift

NO IT

Written and crafted by Jack Keely, Laura Stickney, Pam Thomson, and Nicole Trollinger
Illustrated by Jeff Shelly

Make-n-Gift It Contents

3   Getting Started

4   Milk Carton Bird Feeders

6   Paper Potpourri Planters

10   Splashy Salts and Flavorful Gloss

12   Magnetic Memos

14   Beautiful Beads

16   3-D Greetings

20   Cereal and Tissue Box Frames

22   Totally Tubular Wrapping Paper

24   Funky Flower Pots

26   "Candy" Soap

28   Marvelous Muffin Tin Monoprint

30   Spongy Gift Bags

32   Follow-It Project Patterns

Getting Started

What's even better than getting an awesome gift? Giving one you made yourself! Make-n-Gift It is crammed with a ton of crafty creations that make perfect presents, and your friends and family will love the handmade treasures you'll learn how to create.

Before you use any tool or material for your crafts, check with a grownup first to make sure it's okay. Also go over the "Get It" list with a grownup before you start your Make-n-Gift It craft so you can get some help gathering your materials. (Sometimes you may need an adult's help with a project, just to be safe.) In addition to your supplies and your grownup, find some old rags or newspapers to cover your workspace—your parents will appreciate it if you keep things clean.

Some supplies in the "Get It" list can be found around your home (such as white glue and scissors), but everything else is readily available at your local art and craft store. And if an activity calls for a special pattern, look to the back of this book, where you'll find a tear-out section of all the patterns you'll need. If you want to make a pattern bigger or smaller to customize your project, ask an adult to help you duplicate it on a photocopier.

Most important, have fun, and let your imagination run wild! The ideas in this book can be just the beginning of your crafty adventures— create your own designs and color schemes to give each project your own personal touch. The more creative you get, the better the gift!

Look for this symbol to let you know when a grownup's help is needed.

⚠ Watch It!
Look for this symbol to let you know when special care or precautions are needed.

Milk Carton Bird Feeders

Leaves, twigs, and twine combine with drink cartons to create a special spot where your feathered friends can dine!

Give the neighborhood birds something to sing about! Add finishing touches like a roof of leaves, additional twigs, or braided twine to make your bird feeder more "homey" before you add seeds and hang it from a tree.

Get It!

Milk or juice cartons
Sticks or twigs
Twine
Acrylic paint
Dishwashing liquid
Sandpaper
Medium paintbrush
Craft knife
Scissors
Hole punch

Imagine It!

A hole punch is not only useful, it's also
a fun way of decorating a project like
this with circular patterns.

⚠ Watch It!

Have a grownup help with
the craft knife.

1

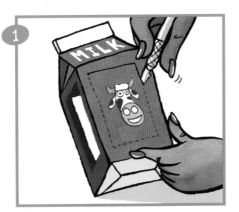

First decide what shape you'd like the opening to
be. Measure it out, and draw it on all four sides of
the carton. Then have a grownup carefully cut out
the four openings with a craft knife.

2

Lightly sandpaper the container, and then paint it
any color you like. (Try adding a drop or two of
dishwashing soap to the paint to help it stick to
the carton.)

3

Make a stencil by cutting out an L-shaped piece of
paper that's the same size as the corner of your
milk carton. Then use a hole punch to make a hole
about halfway down from the inside of the "L."

4

Use the stencil to mark 2 holes below the window
of the bird feeder. Then mark these holes in the
same place on the opposite side of the feeder.
Punch out the 4 holes for your perches.

5

Push 2 long sticks through the holes on both sides
of the feeder. Use twine to tie on small sticks at
the front and back of the perches.

6

Have a grownup poke 2 holes in the top of the
container so you can add a handle. Thread a piece
of twine through the holes, and tie a knot.

Paper Potpourri Planters

Recycle old paper to make new fun with these projects for the house—inside and out!

Hearts and stars are just the beginning—you can concoct a whole world of gifts and trinkets with handmade paper pulp!

Get It!

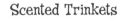

1 cup (250 ml) paper pieces (100% cotton is best), torn to about 1" (2.5 cm) in size

3 cups (750 ml) water

Large mixing bowl

Candy molds or soap molds

Kitchen blender

Hand strainer

White craft glue

Thick, sharp needle or the point of a compass

Ribbon or embroidery thread

Small fabric flower heads

Dried lavender flower petals or cotton balls with scented oil

⚠ Watch It!
Have a grownup help with the sharp needle.

Scented Trinkets

1 Put the paper pieces and water into the blender. Let them sit for 10 minutes. Then pulse (or turn blender on and off) repeatedly until paper dissolves into a fiber pulp.

2 Hold a hand strainer over a bowl, and pour the paper pulp into the strainer. Let most of the moisture drain out into the bowl below before moving to the next step.

3 Place a small amount of the pulp into each mold. Using your fingers, press the pulp down into a thin layer in the mold cups, and then make an indented space in the center of each, just big enough to hold a cotton ball.

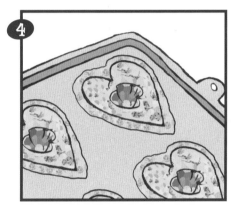

4 Let the pulp flow over the edge of the mold cups at least ¼" (6 mm) to make a ragged edge around the shape. This edge will hold the shapes together later. Let dry 2-3 days; time will vary depending on the size and thickness of the pulp.

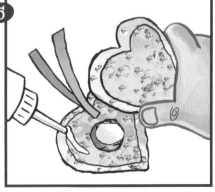

5 Glue a ribbon loop inside the shape at the top; then fill the indent with dried lavender or a cotton ball dotted with scented oil. Glue the halves together and let dry.

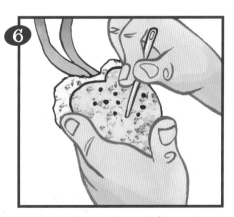

6 Pierce the trinket with the needle (be careful not to pierce yourself!), making random holes to release the scent. Decorate with a fabric flower or bow at the base of the loop.

Get It!

1 cup (250 ml) paper pieces
   (100% cotton is best),
   torn to about 1" (2.5 cm) in size

3 cups (750 ml) water

Large mixing bowl

Candy mold or soap molds

Kitchen blender

Hand strainer

Thick, sharp needle or
   the point of a compass

Ribbon or embroidery thread

Metallic acrylic paint

Medium paintbrush

⚠ Watch It!

Have a grownup help
with the sharp needle.

Star Trinkets

1 Blend the paper pieces and the water in a blender, and then strain the moisture out of the pulp according to the directions in steps 1 and 2 on page 7 (Scented Trinkets).

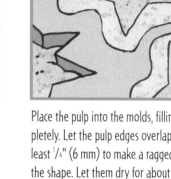

2 Place the pulp into the molds, filling each completely. Let the pulp edges overlap the mold at least ¹/₄" (6 mm) to make a ragged edge around the shape. Let them dry for about 2–3 days.

3 Poke holes into the ragged edge of the dried piece with the needle. Then paint the shape with metallic paint.

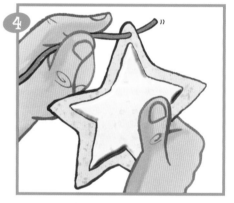

4 String the trinket through the needle hole with ribbon or embroidery thread, and hang it as a decoration or use it as a gift tag.

Get It!

1 cup (250 ml) paper pieces
(100% cotton is best),
torn to about 1" (2.5 cm) in size
3 cups (750 ml) water
Large mixing bowl
Cookie cutters
Kitchen blender
Hand strainer and
flat (paper-making) screen
Thick, sharp needle or
the point of a compass
Ribbon or embroidery thread
Dried flower petals
3 packets wildflower seeds

Watch It!

Have a grownup help
with the sharp needle.

Flower Surprise Packets

1

Follow step 1 on page 7, but make the pulp using same-colored paper scraps. Add some seeds and petals to the finished pulp before straining.

2

Pour the pulp into cookie cutters laid out on a flat screen in the sink. Keep refilling the shapes to the top as the water drains and the paper settles.

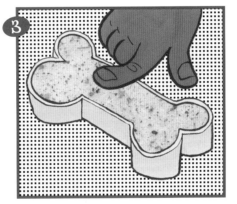

3

When the cookie cutters are full, sprinkle more seeds and flower petals on the wet surface, and tap them into the pulp. Let the pulp drain over the sink for 2–4 days.

4

When dry, poke a hole through the top of each shape with the needle, and then tie a ribbon through the hole. Write planting directions on a tag, and then use your creation or give it away.

Imagine It!

If you use a food dehydrator, these tags will take only 4–8 hours to dry completely.

5

Plant the packet 1/2" (1.5 cm) deep in soft soil, and water daily until shoots appear. Then water as instructed on the seed packet.

Splashy Salts and Flavorful Gloss

When you follow these super-easy recipes, you'll be whipping up a simply beautiful batch of fun and relaxation!

Small jars are perfect containers for fun and fruity lip gloss concoctions. Decorate them with flowers, puffy paint, ribbon roses, or even glitter and jewels to make your lip gloss really shine!

For a great gift, make a single-bath-sized sachet using a small fabric bag tied with ribbon.

Get It!

1 cup (250 ml) coarse rock salt
Food coloring
Scented oil
4 test tubes
4 cork stoppers (for the test tubes)
Mixing spoon
Small mixing bowl
Funnel
Ribbon roses
Ribbon
White craft glue
Pen
Small round, self-stick labels or gift tags

⚠ Watch It!

The melted oil will be hot!
Ask a grownup to help you pour it.

Get it!

2 ounces (60 g) powdered
    drink mix
2 tablespoons (30 ml) solid
    vegetable shortening
Pill box or small container with lid
Microwave-safe pitcher
Assorted ribbons and ribbon roses
White craft glue
Mixing spoon

Scented Bath Crystals

In a bowl, use a spoon to mix the salt together with 3-4 drops of food coloring, or as much as you need to get the color you want. Add 5 drops of scented oil and mix well.

Using the funnel, pour the salts into the test tubes and insert the corks. Tie some ribbon around the top of the test tube, and glue the knot to the glass. Glue a ribbon rose on top of the knot.

Write, "Two tablespoons per bath" ("30 ml per bath") on a round label or gift tag, and stick or glue it to the top of the cork stopper.

Flavored Lip Gloss

Stir the drink mix and the shortening together, and microwave the mixture on high until it is completely melted (30-60 seconds).

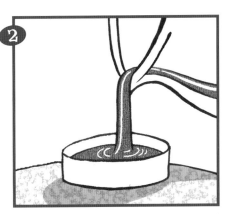

Pour the mixture into the container, and let it cool until it's solid again. Decorate the lid by using glue to attach ribbon and roses.

Magnetic Memos

Scrap paper never looked so stylish as with these "attractive" magnetic notepads!

Bugs and beehives make cool notepads too! See page 35 for the patterns to make these super-cute designs.

Get It!

Photo frame pattern with
   tropical flower pattern (page 33)
8½" x 11" (21 cm x 29.5 cm)
   blue card stock
8½" x 11" (21 cm x 29.5 cm)
   white label paper or contact paper
Picture or photograph
12–16 sheets plain paper, at least 5" x 5"
   (12.5 cm x 12.5 cm)
Magnet
Small brad
White craft glue
Scissors
Hole punch
Craft knife
Ruler

Photo Frame Memo Pad

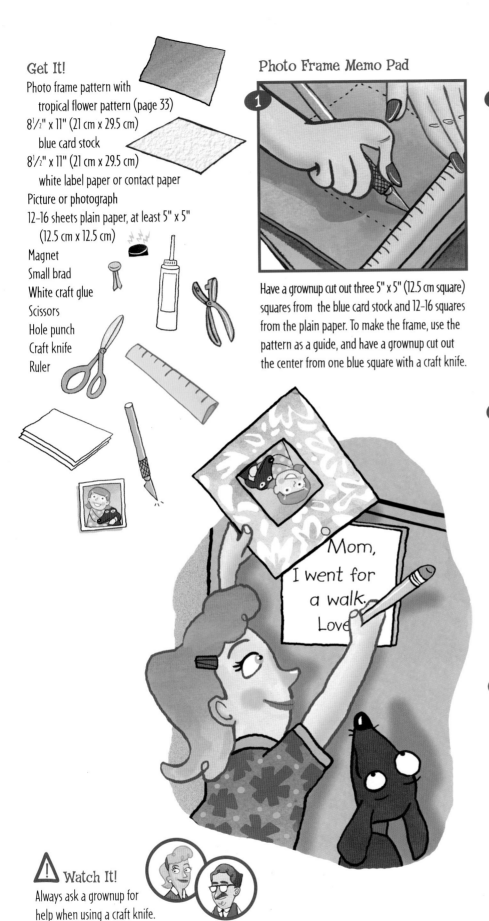

1 Have a grownup cut out three 5" x 5" (12.5 cm square) squares from the blue card stock and 12–16 squares from the plain paper. To make the frame, use the pattern as a guide, and have a grownup cut out the center from one blue square with a craft knife.

2 Use a pencil to trace the flowered pattern onto the label paper. Then cut out the shapes with scissors. Follow the pattern, and stick the shapes onto the frame. Trim away any excess label paper from the inside of the frame.

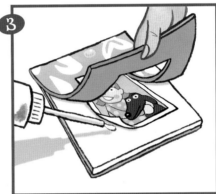

3 Glue the picture to the second blue square so it shows through the window on the first. Then glue the first square on top of the second.

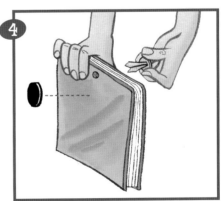

4 Punch holes at the top of all the papers. Secure the frame, paper, and the third blue square with a brad. Glue the magnet to the back.

Mom,
I went for
a walk.
Love

⚠ **Watch It!**
Always ask a grownup for
help when using a craft knife.

Beautiful Beads

Transform magazines or fancy paper into a wonderful variety of bead necklaces, bracelets, and earrings in minutes!

You can make these beautiful beaded masterpieces when you mix scraps of colorful paper with store-bought beads.

Shell-shaped bead

Bugle-shaped bead

Macaroni-shaped bead

Get It!

Bead patterns (page 37)

Decorative paper (such as stationery, magazine pages, or wrapping paper)

Assorted cordings (like plastic lacing, embroidery thread, or elastic)

Assorted jewelry findings (such as jump rings, clasps, or earring studs)

White glue

Bamboo skewer or knitting needle

Scissors

Pencil

Shell-Shaped Bead

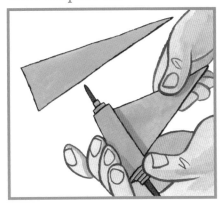

Cut out the pattern from decorative paper. Start at the wide end of the triangle, and roll the paper around the knitting needle, letting it get thicker around the center. When you reach the tip, dab glue on the back, and press it down until dry.

Bugle-Shaped Bead

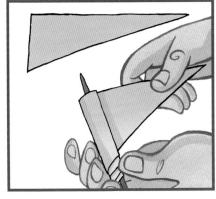

Use the pattern to cut a triangle from decorative paper. Begin rolling around the knitting needle, wide end first. Keep the top edge straight to create the overlapping design. When you reach the tip, glue it down and hold in place until dry.

Macaroni-Shaped Bead

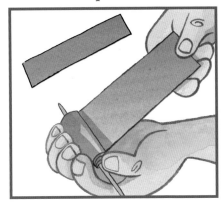

Cut rectangular strips of decorative paper by following the pattern. Start at either end, and keep the edges straight while you roll the strip around the knitting needle. Glue the end of the roll, and press down until dry.

Stringing the Beads

String the beads onto cording to make necklaces and bracelets, or use other jewelry findings for earrings. To create your own unique jewelry, use as many or as few beads as you like. You can even combine different styles or add extra beads.

Imagine It!

You won't have to worry about drying time if you use adhesive-backed paper (such as contact paper) instead of paper and glue. Be sure to leave 1/4" (6 mm) of backing at the starting edge of the triangle to keep the paper from sticking to the tool.

Take:8
Scene:36

3-D Greetings

These funky cards and envelopes are out of this world—you could even say they're from another dimension!

This is a real "window" of opportunity to use your imagination—with cards for any occasion!

Get It!

Window card pattern (page 39)

8½" x 11" (21 cm x 29.5 cm) colored card stock (or substitute heavy colored paper)

Decorative paper (such as stationery, wallpaper, or wrapping paper)

Stickers

White glue

Craft knife

Cutting board (or substitute thick cardboard)

Standard business envelope

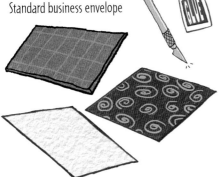

⚠ **Watch It!**
Always ask a grownup for help when using a craft knife.

Window Card

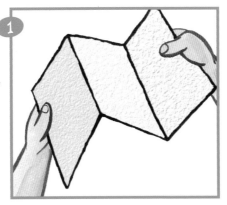

1 Fold the long side of the card stock paper accordion style to create a folded card with three separate panels.

2 Trace the window pattern onto a piece of decorative paper. Make sure the paper is a little larger than the folded card panel.

3 Center the decorative paper over the top panel of the card, and glue it in place. (Some extra paper will hang over the panel's edge.) Smooth out any air bubbles with your hand, and then let it dry.

4 Ask a grownup to use a craft knife to cut out the windows through both the paper and the top panel of the card. Then ask a grownup to trim the excess paper off the sides with the craft knife.

5 Place three stickers on the panel behind the cutout windows, being sure to place them so they can be seen through the holes.

6 Glue the top panel to the panel behind it. Press together, and then let the card dry before writing your message inside.

Get It!

Flower pattern (page 39)

2 pieces 8½" x 11" (21 cm x 29.5 cm) colored card stock (or substitute heavy colored paper)

Cotton makeup pads, cotton balls, or toilet paper

4" x 4" (10 cm x 10 cm) scrap of fabric (any color or style)

12" (30 cm) rickrack

Scraps of green paper

Craft knife

White glue

Decorative scissors

Regular scissors

Ruler

Cutting board (or substitute thick cardboard)

Standard gift card envelope

⚠ **Watch It!**
Always ask a grownup for help when using a craft knife.

Flower Card

Cut one piece of card stock to 6½" x 9" (16.5 cm x 22.5 cm) and the other to 5" x 7½" (12.5 cm x 19 cm). Fold the larger piece in half to create a horizontal card. Then trim ½" (1.5 cm) off the bottom of the top flap with decorative scissors.

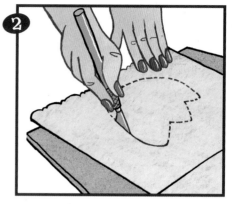

Cut out the flower pattern. Center the pattern on the top flap of the card, and use a pencil to trace around it. Ask a grownup to cut out the area within the tracing with a craft knife, creating a flower-shaped window in the top panel of the card.

Next use the pattern again to cut out the flower shape from 1–3 cotton pads or several sheets of toilet paper. The more pads or paper you use, the thicker the cushion will be. (You can also use cotton balls for the padding instead.)

Place a square of fabric over the window on the back of the front panel of the card, and then glue its edges to the card. The fabric should not be glued too tightly against the card or the padding will not have room to "plump."

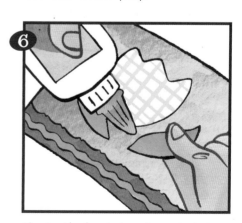

Place the padding over the fabric. Glue the second piece of card stock to the flap, over the padding and fabric. When dry, trim away any excess paper.

Glue the rickrack to the lower flap so that it shows when the card is shut. Glue on leaves cut out from green paper. Let the card dry before writing inside.

Get It!

2 pieces 8½" x 11"
   (21 cm x 29.5 cm)
   card stock in contrasting colors
   (or substitute heavy colored paper)
Confetti
Small balloon
Stickers
3" x 4" (7.5 cm x 10 cm)
   plastic sandwich bag
Craft knife
White glue
Scissors
Ruler
Cutting board (or substitute
   thick cardboard)
Standard gift card envelope

⚠ Watch It!

Always ask a grownup for
help when using a craft knife.

Confetti Card

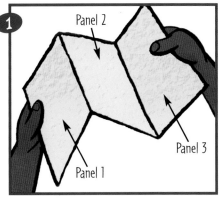

1 Panel 2 — Panel 1 — Panel 3

Cut one color of card stock to 6½" x 13½" (16.5 cm x 34 cm) and the other color to 5½" x 7½" (14 cm x 19 cm). Fold the long side of the larger card accordion style into three panels. Set the smaller panel aside until step 3.

2 Ask a grownup to use a craft knife to cut a 2½" x 3½" (6.5 cm x 9 cm) window out of the first panel (as shown). Position the window 1¼" (3 cm) down from the top and centered on the sides of the front panel.

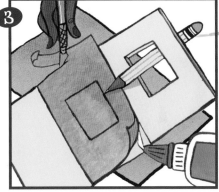

3 Flip the card over, and paste the small panel on top of the second panel, underneath the window of the first. Then trace the rectangle shape of the window onto the paper below. Ask a grownup to use a craft knife to trim away any extra paper beyond the panel's edge.

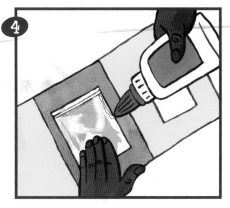

4 Glue around the outline of the rectangle tracing. Then center the plastic bag over the glue (with the opening at top), and press it down along the edges. Check to make sure that the opening at the top of the bag is not glued closed, and then let the glue dry.

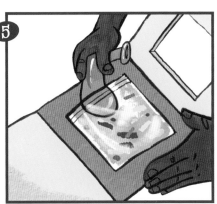

5 Press the stickers inside the bag, and arrange the confetti and the balloon. Then glue the top of the bag closed.

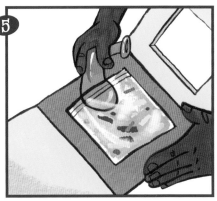

6 Glue the top panel to the second panel. Next glue confetti on the front. Let it dry before you write your message inside.

Cereal and Tissue Box Frames

Home Sweet Home never looked so doggone cute as with these picture-perfect photo frames!

FIDO

How can you make your own house? By putting together discarded materials from around your home. Any big box will work for a frame, and toothpaste boxes make great chimneys. Get creative and decorate your house anyway that you like!

Get It!

3 square, vanity-sized tissue boxes
Cardboard cereal box
White craft glue
Poster paint
Medium paintbrush
Scissors

Imagine It!

When gluing together flat areas, such as shingles or wood trim, use a paper clip to hold it in place while it dries.

Doghouse

Cut out an arched doorway from the front of one of the tissue boxes. Then cut out a second arch from the back, leaving it connected to the box on one side. Next cut a second tissue box in half diagonally, creating a triangular section for the roof.

Cut out pieces from the third tissue box that are the same size as the doghouse's walls. Glue them to the sides of the doghouse, with the shiny side turned in. When dry, paint the doghouse any color you choose.

Cut out 4 strips to use as corner pieces; they should be the height of your doghouse's walls and 1/2" (1.5 cm) wide. Score them lightly by running the blade of your scissors along a ruler placed down the middle of the strip.

Glue the roof on top of the doghouse. Then fold the 4 strips in half, with the scored side on the outside. Paint them, let dry, then glue them to the corners of the doghouse. Repeat to make a step at the base of the front door and a seam for the roof.

Glue the seam to the roof. Cut out 1" (2.5 cm) wide cardboard strips a little longer than the roof. Cut waves in the strips, and glue them to the roof.

Cut a bone shape from a cereal box. Glue squares of cardboard to the back of the bone. Glue the bone to the house.

Cut out and create a 3-sided section of tissue box, as shown. Attach a picture of your dog to the front, and put it in the doghouse.

When you design your own wrapping paper, you're sure to be the hit of the party!

Choosing bright paint colors (or even metallics) to print your papers will make your presents stand out in a crowd!

Get It!

Toilet paper tubes, paper towel tubes, or other cardboard tubes

Scissors

Pencil

White glue

Glue brush

String, cords, or yarn

Tempera or poster paint

Paintbrushes

Papers to print on (such as brown or white butcher paper or thin colored paper)

Imagine It!

Try twisting or braiding pieces of yarn and string to get all sorts of fun and unique prints!

1 Cut a slit in one end of a tube, and insert one end of a long piece of string. Wrap the string tightly around the tube in a random pattern. When you get to the end, make another slit in the tube, and secure the end of the string.

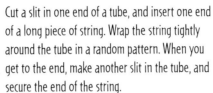

2 You can create a different pattern by brushing glue all over a tube and pressing pieces of yarn around it. Experiment with the spacing between the pieces of yarn as you glue them into place. Allow the tubes to dry overnight.

3 Put some tempera paint (make sure it's not lumpy) into a dish. Brush paint over the string or yarn pattern on the tube, making sure to cover the entire pattern.

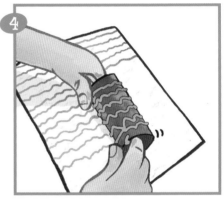

4 Hold the tube by the edges, and roll it all over your paper. Reapply color after each roll. Let your designs overlap, and see what cool patterns you can create!

Funky Flower Pots

You can also paint the entire clay pot with flowery garden designs or decorate it with ribbons, jewels, fabric, or colorful paper!

Get It!

Terra cotta pot
Food coloring (yellow, green, and blue)
Uncooked elbow macaroni
Uncooked rice
Plastic sandwich bags
Paper cups
Pie tin
White craft glue
Silk daisies

Daisy Flower Pot

1 Fill a plastic sandwich bag with ½ cup (125 ml) of rice. Squeeze in a few drops of yellow food coloring, and squeeze and shake the bag until the rice is colored. Do the same to the macaroni, using blue and green food coloring.

2 Pour the colored rice and macaroni into separate paper cups. Draw a wavy design with glue around the top rim and bottom of the pot. Then sprinkle the yellow rice on the wet glue, pressing it into the glue by hand as you go around.

3 Put a little glue into a pie tin. Pick up the colored macaroni, one by one, and dip them into the glue. Make wavy daisy stems by alternating the directions of the noodles as you glue them on. Keep about 2" (5 cm) between each stem.

4 Now choose some daisies that fit onto the rim of your pot. Pull each daisy off its stem, and then cut off as much of the plastic behind the flower as possible (so it will lie flat on the rim). Glue the flowers around the rim.

Imagine It!

Plant different pasta on your pot to make kookier creations. Make waves with an ocean scene using egg noodles and shell pasta, or spell out a colorful story with alphabet pasta!

"Candy" Soap

Make glycerin soaps that look good enough to eat! These petal-perfect gifts are great for washing—but not for snacking!

You can make store-bought soap pretty too! Cover the smooth side with water-based glue sealer. When dry, stencil designs using acrylic craft paint.

You can also pour soap into a shallow pan to cut out cool shapes with cookie cutters!

Get It!

2-pound (1 kg) brick of glycerin soap

Small soap molds or candy molds

Food coloring

1-pint (500 ml) microwave-safe
    measuring cup

Tiny silk flower heads
    (plastic backing removed)

Large silk flower
    (plastic backing removed)

Paper candy cups

Decorative box

Ribbon

Toothpick

Kitchen knife

Mixing spoon

White craft glue

Scented oil or soap fragrance (optional)

1 Have a grownup help you cut five 1" (2.5 cm) cubes from the glycerin brick and place them in the measuring cup. Microwave on high for 40 seconds. Continue to heat for 10 seconds at a time until the soap is completely melted.

2 To make colored shapes, stir the food coloring into the melted soap before pouring the soap into the molds. If you want to make your soaps scented, you can add 2-4 drops of scented oil or soap fragrance now.

3 Fill the molds halfway with melted soap. Place the flower heads face down in the poured soap, and use a toothpick to push the heads half-way down into the soap. Pour in more melted soap to fill the mold. Let cool for 20-30 minutes.

4 Apply gentle pressure to the front of the mold to release the soap shapes. Place each of the finished shapes into a candy cup, and arrange the soaps however you like in the bottom of your decorative box.

5 Lay the ribbon across the box lid. Fold both ends under the box lip, and secure it with glue. Trim off any excess, and then glue the flower on top.

⚠ **Watch It!**
- Melted soap will be very hot! Ask a grownup to help you pour.
- No matter how yummy these soaps look, they should never be eaten!

Marvelous Muffin Tin Monoprint

Whether you keep this book all tied up or hang it on the wall, your printed pages will impress any cook!

Write your favorite recipes neatly on index cards to match your recipe book. Include some family favorites to make it a colorful keepsake!

Get It!

Cherry pattern (page 33)
Small metal muffin tin
 (washed to remove
 any grease)
Poster paint
Paintbrushes
Containers for paint and water
3 pieces of 6 ¼" x 7 ½" (16 cm x 19 cm)
 colored paper
Glue stick
Scissors
Popsicle™ stick
6" x 35" (15 cm x 87.5 cm) paper strip
2 pieces 5" x 6 ½" (12.5 cm x 16 cm) mat
 board or cardboard
Thin ribbon or cord
Hole punch
Eight 4" x 5 ¼" (10 cm x 13 cm) envelopes
Eight 3" x 5" (7.5 cm x 12.5 cm) index cards

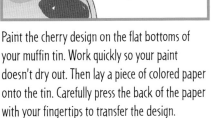

1 Paint the cherry design on the flat bottoms of your muffin tin. Work quickly so your paint doesn't dry out. Then lay a piece of colored paper onto the tin. Carefully press the back of the paper with your fingertips to transfer the design.

2 Gently peel the paper off the tin and set it aside to dry. You'll need to make at least three sheets. (Keep your favorites for the covers!) Each time you print, repaint your tin with the pattern. Then let everything dry.

3 Lay one sheet of your printed paper face down. Glue the paper to a cardboard piece, leaving an edge around the board. Smooth it out, and then glue the other cover together. Now trim the corners, and glue the edges down. Let the covers dry.

4 Cut off the top flaps of your envelopes. Cut out some cherry circles from your extra prints, and glue them to your envelopes. Fold the long strip of paper in half, and then fold it in half twice more, creasing each fold with a Popsicle stick.

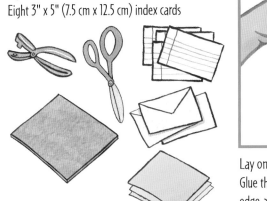

5 Open up the strip, and refold as shown (accordion style). Glue the top and bottom panels of the paper to the covers, centering them carefully.

6 Now glue the envelopes onto the paper as shown. Punch a hole in the top cover, and attach a ribbon. Fill the envelopes with your favorite recipes!

Spongy Gift Bags

Make any gift extra special by stashing it in one of these colorfully printed bags!

You can use old kitchen sponges for your stamps; just make sure they're clean (and don't forget to ask a grownup if it's okay).

Get It!

Permanent marker
Sponges
Scissors
Poster paint
Paintbrush
Blank shopping bags with handles
Cardstock, smaller than a lunch bag
Hole punch
Ribbon
Brown lunch bags

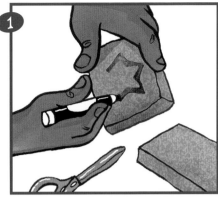

1 Draw some simple shapes onto dry sponges with a permanent marker, and cut them out. If a sponge is hard to cut, wet it slightly, and pinch the sponge as you cut.

2 Brush some paint onto a sponge shape. Stamp your shape onto one side of a blank bag. Now let the printed side of the bag dry completely before you print the second side.

3 Create a gift tag by stamping onto a small piece of cardstock. Let it dry, and then fold the card in half. Punch a hole in the corner, and attach it to your gift bag handle with a ribbon.

4 You can also make a gift bag out of a sandwich bag by printing on a separate piece of cardstock and gluing it to the bag. Cut the edges with wavy scissors and add ribbon!

Imagine It!

Who says you have to stick to shapes? You could also trace and cut out some sponge letters—then stamp out a name or a phrase (like "Happy Birthday!" or "Let's Celebrate!").

Follow-It Project Patterns

This is where you'll find a special tear-out section of all the patterns you'll need. If you want to make a pattern bigger or smaller to customize your project, ask a grownup to help you to enlarge or reduce it on a photocopier.

Walter Foster®

Walter Foster Publishing, Inc.
23062 La Cadena Drive
Laguna Hills, California 92653
www.walterfoster.com
© 2002 Walter Foster Publishing, Inc.
All rights reserved.

Special thanks to Stephanie Sarracino and the students at Bonita Canyon Elementary School
and to Robyn Allen and the students at Huntington Seacliff Elementary School for their contributions as craft consultants.

Order Code: IT06
ISBN: 1-56010-652-2
UPC: 0-50283-86406-6

Produced by the creative team at Walter Foster Publishing, Inc.:
Sydney Sprague, Associate Publisher
Pauline Foster, Art Director/Designer
Barbara Kimmel, Senior Editor
Samantha Chagollan and Jenna Winterberg, Editors
Carole Thorpe, Production Designer
Toni Gardner, Production Manager
Kathy Beeler, Production Coordinator
Monica Noemi Mijares-DeCuir, Production Artist

Printed in Korea.

Photo Frame Memo Pad Pattern with Tropical Flower Pattern (Pages 12-13)

Muffin Tin Cherry Pattern (Pages 28-29)

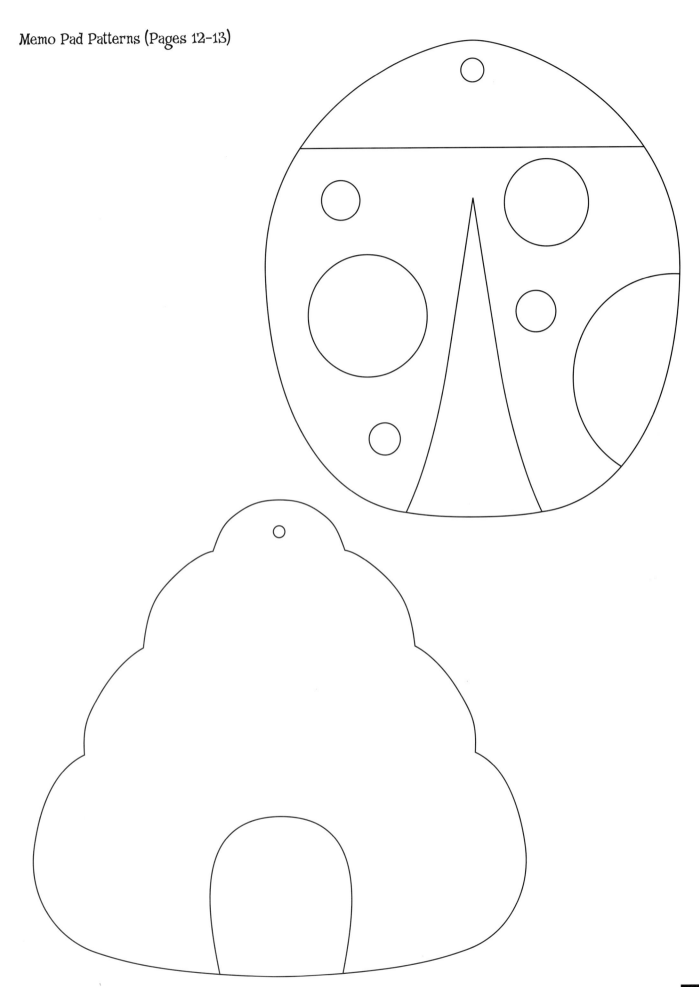

Macaroni-Shaped Bead

Bugle-Shaped Bead

Shell-Shaped Bead

Window Card Pattern (pages 16-17)

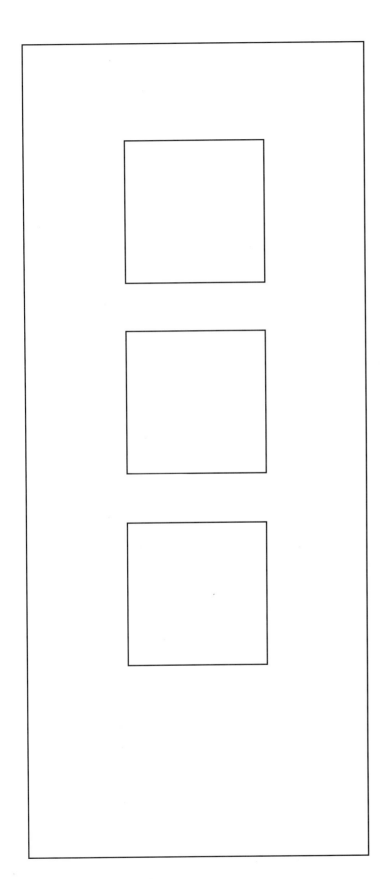

Flower Pattern (Pages 16-18)